D1685977

TRANQUILLITY

Rainforests are places of exquisite beauty. A myriad waterways, waterfalls and rapids abound, fed by the constant rain, lifeblood of the forest. A cascade will slowly undercut the rock ledge over which it tumbles, and so it very gradually moves upstream.

The noise of rushing water fills the air; misty spray feeding the mosses, ferns and lichens that grow on rocks and tree trunks.

Opposite:

Russell Falls in Tasmania's Mt Field National Park

Left:

Rainforest, Mt Warning, New South Wales

RAINFOREST GIANTS

The Strangler Fig relies on birds and other rainforest giants for its life. Birds eat its fruit and disperse the seed, which can only shoot high up in the forest canopy on a host tree. The young fig sends roots down to the ground, and gradually grows all around the host, strangling it by depriving it of light and nutrients. Slowly the host succumbs, leaving a stalwart fig to take its place in the forest.

The Antarctic Beech is a link with the time when Australia was part of the southern super-continent called Gondwana. The trees' lifespan may be as much as 3000 years, and their remote ancestors were becoming established at the end of the age of dinosaurs. These were among the first flowering plants and, in the beginning, beech forests were widespread in Australia. Today, climate changes have confined the beech to temperate spots with heavy, reliable rainfall.

Opposite:
A Strangler Fig on a host tree

Right:
Antarctic Beech, Lamington National Park, Queensland

Steve Parish

DISCOVERING AUSTRALIAN
RAINFORESTS

A LITTLE AUSTRALIAN GIFT BOOK

www.steveparish.com.au

DISCOVERING RAINFORESTS

For millions of years, rainforests covered much of the surface of Australia. Over more millions of years, as the continent became increasingly arid, they shrank in size, a process hastened in the past two centuries by human activities.

Today, Australia's rainforests exist mainly in the wetter areas of north-eastern and south-eastern Australia. The country harbours wet tropical, warm temperate and cool temperate rainforests. Most are National Parks, and many have been listed as World Heritage Areas.

For best growth, a temperate or tropical rainforest needs to receive at least 1300 mm of rainfall each year, preferably spread evenly over the 12 months. One-quarter is used by the forest, while the rest returns to the air, to float above the forest as cloud, shielding the Earth beneath from the Sun's rays. When the cloud carries enough water and the temperature drops, rain falls once again.

Rainforests are alive with animals, many of them living in the leafy branches crowning the tall-trunked trees. In this book, Steve Parish has gathered images of Australia's rainforests with their majestic trees and waterfalls, and of the plants and animals which make them so special.

Front cover:

Nandroya Falls, Wooroonooran National Park, Queensland

Opposite:

"The Ballroom", Cradle Mountain-Lake St Claire National Park, Tasmania

BOTANICAL GLORIES

The Crows Nest Fern is just one of the rainforest plants that grow aloft on trunks and branches to reach for light. Although these species are called "shade tolerant", all plants need light to function. Within the leaves are tiny green particles of chlorophyll that are powered by sunlight to turn minerals and water into food that the plant uses for growth and maintenance.

The leaves of ferns and palms spread to catch and make the most of the sunlight filtering through the forest canopy.

Opposite:
Alexandra Palms, Eungella National Park, Queensland

Left:
Crows Nest Fern growing on a tree stump

PALMS AND FERNS

Both palms and ferns occur in tropical and subtropical rainforests, but the ferns, especially tree ferns, come into their own in temperate rainforests.

Ferns have a fossil history going back 350 million years, being most prominent in Australia about 250 million years ago. Australia now has about 430 species of fern, compared with its more than 20 000 species of flowering plants.

Fan Palms grow in a few rainforest locations in far north Queensland, and are an intrinsic part of the habitat of the highly threatened Southern Cassowary.

Opposite:
Tree ferns in a Tasmanian gully

Left:
Fan Palms, northern Queensland

FLORAL SPLENDOUR

Flowers sprout from the trunk of the Bumpy Satinash (below), offering conveniently placed nectar to bats, gliders and insects. Rainforest trees depend on the animals and insects for pollination, and their flowers are brightly coloured to attract attention. As this consumes a great deal of energy, many trees do not flower until they are 30 or 40 years old, when they may only flower every third or fourth year.

The elegant Cooktown Orchid (opposite) is the floral emblem of the State of Queensland.

Opposite:
**Queensland's
floral emblem,
the Cooktown
Orchid**

Right:
**The Bumpy
Satinash's
flowering
trunk**

FUNGI

In rainforests of all types, dead wood in fallen trees is broken down with the help of fungi. These fascinating plants are everywhere — moulds, yeasts, mildews, toadstools, mushrooms, puffballs and a host of others, both beautiful and grotesque. Having no chlorophyll, fungi cannot use the sun's energy to manufacture food, so some exist as parasites while others feed on dead plants. The part of the fungus that is visible is its fruiting body, which contains spores. Less easily found are the hyphae, threads in a fine network spreading throughout the food source, busily gathering nourishment.

Opposite:
A fallen tree, prime habitat for fungi, in Tasmania's forests

Left:
A fan-like Bracket Fungus

RAINFOREST EXPERIENCE

The forest stands guard around us,

calm and still.

Before us, the waterfall

spills in silver splendour

over fern-draped terraces.

We share

the songs of the forest

in a closeness of spirit

that needs no words.

Together we dream, hope, imagine.

In the forest each of us finds

our heart's desire.

Opposite:

Chalahn Falls,

Lamington

National Park

Right:

Capturing the

experience

SUPERB SONGSTER

In late winter, the temperate rainforest of south-eastern Australia resounds to the mimicry and song of the male Superb Lyrebird. Shimmering tail outspread, he dances and sings to attract females willing to be wooed and won.

Opposite:
Fern gullies are an ideal habitat for the Superb Lyrebird.

Left:
Superb Lyrebird

RAINFOREST FROGS

Frogs flourish in the humid rainforest, which is full of small, frog-friendly habitats. They crouch on leaves, float in water-filled holes in tree trunks, swim in streams and leap around in the leaf litter, being both predator and prey. They eat insects and are, in turn, eaten by snakes, lizards, birds — and other frogs. Frogs are an early warning system for the rainforest. If they are abundant, all is well. If frogs begin to disappear, we should examine the well-being of their home.

Opposite and left:

The Red-eyed Tree Frog lives high in the canopy, coming to the ground after rain to breed.

THE WATERFALL

Silver water

spills like veils of lace

over shining rocks

into the pool beneath.

Rings of ripples

chase each other

across the shining water.

An azure kingfisher swoops upon

an emerald dragonfly.

This is rainforest beauty.

Opposite:
Nandroya Falls,
Wooroonooran
National Park,
north
Queensland

Right:
Elabana Falls,
Lamington
National Park,
Queensland

THE BIRDS

Australia's northern rainforests are home to many different birds. This abundance is possible because the forests offer so many places to feed: flower nectar, fruit and insects in the canopy; insects, spiders, lizards, frogs and other food on the tree trunks, vines, creepers and shrubbier trees of the lower storey; the small crawling creatures like worms, snails, centipedes and insects of the ground litter.

In 1868 the poet Henry Kendall wrote, "All day long these deep, grand solitudes are ringing with the varied voices of their innumerable feathered denizens…gorgeous parrots among the taller saplings, leaping from bough to bough like living jets of crimson flame…". However, the brilliant colours of the female Eclectus Parrot (below left) and Crimson Rosella (below right) blend into the greens, coppery reds and blue shadows of the forest canopy.

Pages 24–25:
Dorrigo National Park, northern New South Wales

Opposite:
In dense rainforest, birds are often heard rather than seen.

Left:
Crimson Rosella

Far left:
Eclectus Parrot

THE SERPENT DREAMING IN THE HEART

Aboriginal Australians told

of a Dreamtime serpent,

maker of mountains,

progenitor of rivers

creator of forests.

Later comers to the southern continent

feared the serpent's children,

coveted the serpent's country,

destroyed forest and forest creatures

with axe and fire.

To some of us, time has brought wisdom.

In the heart of the disappearing forest,

where the serpent dreams

of green beauty recovering the land,

we stand in wonder, sharing the dream.

Opposite:

**The magic of
rainforest**

Left:

**Green Tree
Snake**

IN PRISTINE STREAMS

Platypus can be found hunting freshwater shrimps and insect larvae in clear, unpolluted water from the tropical rainforest lowlands of north Queensland to the cool temperate forests of Tasmania. The platypus closes its eyes, ears and nostrils when it dives, detecting its prey with its sensitive, rubbery bill. It stores its food in its cheek-pouches until it surfaces to eat.

The female digs a nest burrow in the stream bank. In a nursery chamber at the end, she lays two round, soft-shelled eggs. These she incubates between her tail and her body. When the young hatch, she suckles them.

Opposite:
Johnstone River, Wooroonooran National Park, north Queensland

Right:
A platypus skims through the water.

INDEX OF FEATURES PICTURED

Right:

In the heart of the forest